CW00370371

asian salads

asian salads

Marshall Cavendish
Cuisine

Editor: Lydia Leong
Designer: Benson Tan
Series Designer: Bernard Go Kwang Meng

Published by Marshall Cavendish Cuisine
An imprint of Marshall Cavendish International
1 New Industrial Road, Singapore 536196

Other Marshall Cavendish Offices:
Marshall Cavendish Ltd.5th Floor, 32–38 Saffron Hill, London EC1N 8FH • Marshall Cavendish Corporation. 99 White Plains
Road, Tarrytown NY 10591-9001, USA • Marshall Cavendish International (Thailand) Co Ltd. 253 Asoke, 12th Flr,
Sukhumvit 21 Road, Klongtoey Nua, Wattana, Bangkok 10110, Thailand • Marshall Cavendish (Malaysia) Sdn Bhd,
Times Subang, Lot 46, Subang Hi-Tech Industrial Park, Batu Tiga, 40000 Shah Alam, Selangor Darul Ehsan, Malaysia

Marshall Cavendish is a trademark of Times Publishing Limited

National Library Board Singapore Cataloguing in Publication Data

Asian salads. – Singapore : Marshall Cavendish Cuisine, c2008.
p. cm. – (Mini cookbooks)
ISBN-13 : 978-981-261-605-0
ISBN-10 : 981-261-605-5

1. Salads. 2. Cookery, Asian. I. Series: Mini cookbooks

TX740
641.83 -- dc22   OCN228039544

Printed in Singapore by Saik Wah Press Pte Ltd

contents

asian
salads

scallop salad Serves 3–4

This light and refreshing scallop dish is not only attractive to the eye, but also tasty. Serve as a starter or side dish.

INGREDIENTS

Scallops on shell	9
Lettuce	a few leaves from heart of lettuce
Onion	1 large, peeled and finely sliced
Coriander leaves (cilantro)	5 sprigs, coarsely chopped

DRESSING

Lemon juice	2 Tbsp
Garlic	2 cloves, peeled and crushed
Bird's eye chillies	2, finely chopped + 3 whole
Salt	to taste
Olive oil	1 Tbsp

METHOD

• Remove scallops from shells and discard tendon. Wash well, then place in a saucepan of cold water. Bring to simmering point and cook gently for 5–10 minutes.

• Wash scallop shells and pat dry. Line with lettuce leaves. Arrange cooked scallops on lettuce with sliced onion and coarsely chopped coriander.

• Combine dressing ingredients in a small sauce bowl. Drizzle dressing over scallops or serve on the side.

papaya salad Serves 2–3

This raw papaya salad is ideal for stimulating the taste buds at the start of a meal, or for cleansing the palate in between courses.

INGREDIENTS

Coarsely grated raw papaya	4–5 cups
Garlic	3 cloves, peeled and chopped
Bird's eye chilies	3, chopped
Thai fish sauce	1 Tbsp
Lemon juice	2 Tbsp
Roasted peanuts	2 Tbsp, crushed
Ground white pepper	to taste
Lettuce leaves	

METHOD

• Toss grated papaya with garlic, chillies, fish sauce, lemon juice and peanuts together in a mixing bowl. Season with pepper.

• Line a serving plate or salad bowl with lettuce leaves. Spoon salad over and garnish as desired. Serve.

vegetable and chicken salad (lawar) Serves 4

Known in Southeast Asia as *lawar*, this Indonesian dish is an interesting combination of young jackfruit, long beans and chicken.

INGREDIENTS

Cooking oil	3 Tbsp
Salam leaves	2
Coconut milk	250 ml (8 fl oz / 1 cup)
Chicken fillet	300 g (11 oz), finely diced
Salt	to taste
Sugar	to taste
Long beans	200 g (7 oz), cut into 0.5-cm ($^{1}/_{4}$-in) lengths
Young jackfruit	300 g (11 oz), peeled, blanched and cut into bite-size pieces
Grated or desiccated coconut	45 g (1 $^{1}/_{2}$ oz), toasted
Crisp-fried shallots	30 g (1 oz)
Bird's eye chillies	6, left whole or finely sliced
Lime juice	to taste

PASTE

Red chillies	5
Black peppercorns	$^{1}/_{2}$ tsp
Candlenuts	3
Shallots	6, peeled
Garlic	4 cloves, peeled
Galangal	1-cm ($^{1}/_{2}$-in) knob, peeled
Turmeric	1-cm ($^{1}/_{2}$-in) knob, peeled
Lemon grass	1 stalk, tough outer leaves removed, ends trimmed and finely sliced
Grated palm sugar	2 Tbsp

METHOD

- Pound ingredients for paste together until fine. Heat oil in a wok and fry paste until fragrant. Add *salam* leaves, coconut milk and chicken. Cook until coconut milk is slightly thick. Season with salt and sugar. Remove from heat and set aside in a serving bowl to cool. Shred chicken when cool and return to bowl.

- Add long beans, jackfruit, coconut, crisp-fried shallots and chillies to bowl. Toss well and season with lime juice. Serve at room temperature.

spicy mackerel salad Serves 2–3

A light but tasty fried fish salad with crushed chillies, peanuts and green apple strips.

INGREDIENTS

Mackerels	4, medium, cleaned
Cooking oil for deep-frying	
Green apple	1
Shallots	4–5, peeled and finely chopped
Ginger	2.5-cm (1-in) knob, peeled and grated
Red chillies	4, lightly crushed
Green chillies	4, lightly crushed
Raw peanuts	3 Tbsp, roasted, skinned and crushed
Lemons	2, grated for 1 Tbsp zest and squeezed for 3 Tbsp juice
Salt	to taste
Freshly ground black pepper	to taste
Lettuce leaves	5

GARNISH
Coriander leaves
(cilantro)

METHOD

• Steam fish for 5–7 minutes until lightly cooked, then remove from steamer and gently pat dry. Heat cooking oil and deep-fry steamed fish until golden. Drain and leave to cool. Debone and skin, then flake flesh.

• Peel apple and finely shred.

• Toss fish meat with shredded apple, shallots, ginger, chillies and peanuts in a mixing bowl. Add lemon juice and zest. Season with salt and pepper to taste. Mix well.

• Dish salad out onto a plate lined with lettuce leaves. Garnish with coriander leaves and serve.

prawn and mango salad Serves 4–6

This Thai salad is sweet, spicy and sour at the same time. To keep the salad from becoming soggy, toss it just before serving.

INGREDIENTS

Freshwater prawns (shrimps)	500 g (1 lb 1 1/2 oz), boiled and drained
Raw mangoes	2, peeled and finely sliced
Kaffir lime leaves	2, finely sliced
Coriander leaves (cilantro)	1 sprig, chopped
Mint leaves	6–8 leaves, chopped
Thai fish sauce	4 Tbsp
Limes	2, juice extracted
Salt	to taste
Sugar	to taste
Glass noodles	200 g (7 oz), soaked in cold water until soft, then drained
Crisp-fried shallots	1 Tbsp
Raw peanuts	2 Tbsp, roasted, skinned and crushed
Lettuce leaves	

PASTE

Red chillies	3
Bird's eye chillies	3
Dried prawns (shrimps)	1 1/2 Tbsp, soaked in water for 20 minutes, then drained
Garlic	3 cloves, peeled
Grated palm sugar or brown sugar	3 Tbsp
Tomatoes	2, medium, cut into quarters

METHOD

• Pound ingredients for paste together until fine.

• Combine all ingredients for salad, except for peanuts and salad greens, and toss well with paste.

• Line a serving dish with lettuce and top with salad. Sprinkle crushed peanuts over and serve immediately.

thai beef salad (yam nua) Serves 4–6

This Thai salad is an interesting combination of flavours and textures. Sweet, spicy and sour, it is simple-to-do, yet extremely tasty.

INGREDIENTS

Sirloin beef steak	500 g (1 lb 1¹/₂ oz)
White onions	2, large, peeled, halved and finely sliced
Coriander leaves (cilantro)	50 g (1²/₃ oz), chopped
Red chilli	1, seeded and cut into thin strips, then soaked in cold water for 30 minutes
Lettuce leaves	

SALAD DRESSING

Garlic	10 cloves, peeled and coarsely chopped
Bird's eye chillies	5, seeded, if desired and coarsely chopped
Thai fish sauce	3 Tbsp
Lemon or lime juice	3 Tbsp
Sugar	2 Tbsp

METHOD

• Grill beef until medium or well done. Leave to cool slightly, then slice thinly. Set beef aside to cool.

• Combine ingredients for salad dressing and mix well. Refrigerate for 30 minutes, or until sufficiently chilled.

• Place sliced beef, onions, coriander leaves and chilli strips in a bowl and toss gently, being careful not to break up beef. Drizzle chilled dressing over salad.

• Line a serving plate with lettuce leaves and arrange salad on leaves. Serve cold.

chicken with mint Serves 4-6

Fresh mint leaves cannot withstand cooking and should only be added at the end of cooking to flavour the dish as done in this recipe.

INGREDIENTS

Chicken breast	600 g (1 lb 5¹/₃ oz), cut into thin strips
Vegetable oil	4 Tbsp
Lemon grass	3 stalks, tough outer leaves removed, ends trimmed and sliced
Salt	to taste
Sugar	to taste
Lime	1, juice extracted
Mint leaves	a handful, chopped

MARINADE

Onion	1, large, peeled
Garlic	4 cloves, peeled
Ginger	1-cm (¹/₂-in) knob, peeled
Thai fish sauce	1 Tbsp
Ground white pepper	1 tsp

PASTE

Red chillies	10, large
Dried prawn (shrimp) paste (*belacan*)	1 Tbsp
Lemon grass	2 stalks, tough outer leaves removed, ends trimmed and sliced
Ginger	1-cm (¹/₂-in) knob, peeled
Garlic	4 cloves, peeled

METHOD

- Combine ingredients for marinade and add chicken. Mix well and refrigerate for at least 2 hours.

- Pound ingredients for paste together until fine. Heat oil in a wok and fry lemon grass for a few minutes. Add paste and continue frying until fragrant.

- Add marinated chicken and fry until chicken is cooked through. Season with salt, sugar and lime juice. Toss in mint leaves just before serving.

vegetable pickle Makes about 800 g (1³/₄ lb)

This crunchy vegetable pickle can be served as an accompaniment to rice dishes.

INGREDIENTS

Cucumbers	300 g (11 oz)
Carrots	150 g (5¹/₃ oz)
Bamboo shoots	150 g (5¹/₃ oz)
Candlenuts	5, roasted
Turmeric	1-cm (¹/₂-in) knob, peeled and chopped
Garlic	2 cloves, peeled
Shallots	4, peeled
Salt	1 tsp
Cooking oil	3 Tbsp
Lemon grass	1 stalk, tough outer leaves removed, ends trimmed and bruised
Screwpine (*pandan*) leaf	1, cut into 5-cm (2-in) pieces
Water	250 ml (8 fl oz / 1 cup)
White vinegar	1–2 tsp
French beans	100 g (3¹/₂ oz), cut into 3-cm (1¹/₄-in) lengths, then slit lengthwise
Raw peanuts	100 g (3¹/₂ oz), boiled and skinned
Bird's eye chillies	10, slit and seeded
Sugar	1–2 Tbsp

METHOD

• Cut cucumbers, carrots and bamboo shoots into 1 x 1 x 3-cm (¹/₂ x ¹/₂ x 1¹/₄-in) pieces. Boil bamboo shoots to remove bitterness.

• Pound candlenuts, turmeric, garlic, shallots and salt together into a fine paste. Heat oil in a wok and sauté paste, lemon grass and screwpine leaf until fragrant. Add water and vinegar and bring to the boil.

• Add cooked bamboo shoots, French beans, carrots, cucumbers, peanuts and bird's eye chillies. Stir in sugar to taste. Remove from heat when ingredients are cooked. Leave to cool, then store refrigerated in an airtight jar. Use as needed.

kimchi Makes about 800 g (1³/₄ lb)

This spicy side dish is consumed by Koreans daily and is perfect with a bowl of plain white rice.

INGREDIENTS

Chinese (napa) cabbage	1 kg (2 lb 3 oz), coarsely chopped
Kosher or pickling salt (non-iodised)	3 Tbsp
Cold water	375 ml (12 fl oz / 1½ cups)
Spring onions (scallions)	4, finely chopped
Ginger	5-cm (2-in) knob, peeled and grated
Dried chilli flakes	1½ tsp
Garlic	4 cloves, peeled and finely chopped
Chilli powder	2 tsp

N o T E

To achieve a fully fermented kimchi, you can also opt to put it in a jar and leave for 3–7 days at room temperature. Store refrigerated.

METHOD

- Place cabbage and salt in a large mixing bowl and mix well. Use a smaller bowl or plate to weigh down cabbage. Set aside for 3 hours at room temperature. Toss the cabbage occasionally during this period.

- Rinse cabbage with cold water, drain and squeeze out as much water as possible.

- Place cabbage and remaining ingredients in an airtight container and mix well. Set aside for 2–3 days in a cool place. Store refrigerated.

soba, mango and cucumber salad Serves 6

Make this cheerful coloured cold salad on a hot day. The sweetness of the mango and the cool crunchiness of the cucumber will be refreshing.

INGREDIENTS

Dried soba	180 g (6 oz)
Tomatoes	2, peeled and cut into small cubes
Cucumber	$^1/_2$, julienned
Mango	1, halved, pitted and thinly sliced
Chopped basil	3 Tbsp
Chopped mint	3 Tbsp
Roasted salted peanuts	100 g ($3^1/_2$ oz), chopped
Limes	2, cut into wedges

DRESSING

Rice vinegar	90 ml (3 fl oz / $^3/_8$ cup)
Sugar	2 Tbsp
Salt	$^1/_2$ tsp
Garlic	1 clove, peeled and chopped
Bird's eye chilli	1, seeded and chopped
Lime	2, grated for zest + squeezed for $1^1/_2$ Tbsp juice
Sesame oil	1 Tbsp

METHOD

• Prepare dressing. Add vinegar, sugar, and salt to a small saucepan. Warm over medium heat, stirring occasionally, for 1 minute or until sugar dissolves. Stir in garlic and chilli. Remove from heat and set aside to cool. Mix in lime zest and juice and sesame oil.

• Bring a pot of salted water to the boil. Add soba and cook until tender but still firm to the bite, stirring occasionally. Drain well. Rinse under cold water and drain well. Transfer soba to large bowl.

• Add dressing to soba, toss and mix evenly.

• Add cucumber, mango, basil and mint to soba and toss well. Arrange salad on a plate. Sprinkle with chopped peanuts and serve with lime wedges.

crispy noodle caesar salad Serves 4

The use of crispy noodles instead of croutons in this recipe gives the classic Caesar Salad an oriental twist. Serve as an appetiser or as an accompaniment to roasted meat dishes.

INGREDIENTS

Cooking oil for deep-frying	
Thin yellow egg noodles	125 g (4½ oz), cut into short lengths
Bacon	3 slices, cut into 2.5-cm (1-in) pieces
Chicken breast fillets	750 g (1 lb 10 oz), halved
Baby cos lettuce	1, cut into 2.5-cm (1-in) wide strips
Eggs	3, hard-boiled, peeled and quartered
Caesar salad dressing	85 ml (2½ fl oz / ⅓ cup)

METHOD

• Heat oil for deep-frying and gently lower in egg noodles. Deep-fry until golden brown. Drain well and set aside. Reserve 1 Tbsp oil.

• Heat reserved oil in a non-stick frying pan over medium-high heat. Add bacon and fry for 3–4 minutes, or until crisp. Drain and set aside.

• In the same pan, add half the chicken. Cook for 3 minutes each side, or until golden brown and cooked through. Drain, set aside and allow to cool. Repeat with remaining chicken. Thinly slice chicken and transfer to a salad bowl.

• Add lettuce leaves to the salad bowl, toss and mix well. Crumble in bacon and crispy noodles and top with eggs.

• Drizzle dressing over salad and serve immediately.

chilli udon chicken salad Serves 2

This is a scrumptious combination of udon, crispy chicken pieces and sweet and spicy chilli sauce. Serve with chilled beer.

INGREDIENTS

Udon	150 g (5 oz)
Thai chilli sauce	4 Tbsp
Bean sprouts	55 g (2 oz), washed and trimmed
Cooking oil for deep-frying	
Chicken breast fillets	2, cubed
Corn flour (cornstarch)	100 g (3 1/2 oz)
Egg white	1, lightly beaten
Spring onions (scallions)	2, thinly sliced
Roasted white sesame seeds	1 tsp

METHOD

• Bring a pot of salted water to the boil. Add udon and cook for 3 minutes. Drain and transfer to a bowl. Add 2 Tbsp chilli sauce and bean sprouts, mix well and set aside.

• Heat oil for deep-frying. Toss chicken pieces in corn flour, then coat with egg white. Gently lower chicken pieces into hot oil. Deep-fry until crisp and golden brown. Drain well.

• Divide noodles and chicken pieces between 2 individual serving bowls. Drizzle with remaining chilli sauce. Garnish with spring onions and sesame seeds and serve immediately.

chinese cold noodles with peanut sauce Serves 4

This dish is a perfect balance of sweet, savoury and spicy flavours.

INGREDIENTS

Thick rice vermicelli	450 g (1 lb)
Sesame oil	2 Tbsp
Cucumber	1/2, medium, seeded, and julienned
Roasted peanuts	85 g (3 oz), chopped
Spring onions (scallions)	2, thinly sliced
Carrot	1, julienned and soaked in iced water

DRESSING

Peanut butter	100 g (3 1/2 oz)
Water	4 Tbsp
Light soy sauce	3 Tbsp
Dark soy sauce	90 ml (3 fl oz / 3/8 cup)
Roasted white sesame seeds	2 Tbsp
Sesame oil	125 ml (4 fl oz / 1/2 cup)
Chinese cooking wine (hua tiao)	2 Tbsp
Rice vinegar	1 1/2 Tbsp
Honey	4 Tbsp
Garlic	4 cloves, peeled and finely chopped
Chopped ginger	2 tsp
Hot water	125 ml (4 fl oz / 1/2 cup)

METHOD

- Bring a large pot of water to the boil. Add noodles and cook until barely tender and still firm. Drain and plunge into cold water. Drain well and toss noodles with sesame oil and transfer to a serving dish.

- Prepare dressing. Combine all ingredients except hot water in a blender until smooth. Add hot water and blend until the consistency of whipping cream.

- Top noodles with cucumber, peanuts, spring onions and carrot. Serve noodles at room temperature with dressing on the side.

cold sesame noodles Serves 4

With the exception of boiling the dried soba, this refreshing bowl of noodles does not require any cooking.

INGREDIENTS

Dried soba	250 g (9 oz)
Honey	4 Tbsp
Rice vinegar	4 Tbsp
Light soy sauce	4 Tbsp
Sesame oil	2 Tbsp
Cos lettuce	½ head, roughly chopped
Cucumber	1, large, seeded and cut into long strips
Carrot	1, peeled and cut into long strips
Ham	225 g (8 oz)
Coriander leaves (cilantro)	6 sprigs, chopped
Roasted white sesame seeds	1 Tbsp

METHOD

• Bring a saucepan of water to the boil over high heat. Add soba and cook, stirring occasionally, for 3–5 minutes or until just tender. Drain, rinse under cold water to cool, and drain again.

• Combine honey, vinegar, soy sauce and oil. Mix well and refrigerate for 30 minutes.

• Place soba in a serving dish and mix with cos lettuce, cucumber, carrot, ham and coriander. Pour chilled dressing over salad. Sprinkle with sesame seeds and serve.

thai glass noodle salad Serves 2–4

This classic Thai salad, *yum woon sen,* has a tangy sauce and is light and refreshing. It is usually served as a side dish, but can also be served as a light main course.

INGREDIENTS

Cooking oil	2 Tbsp
Minced pork	200 g (7 oz)
Bird's eye chilli	1, seeded and chopped
Bean sprouts	300 g (11 oz), chopped
Spring onions (scallions)	3, finely chopped
Glass (transparent) noodles	200 g (7 oz), soaked to soften, then cut into 5-cm (2-in) lengths
Chopped roasted peanuts	2 Tbsp
Coriander leaves (cilantro)	1 sprig

SAUCE

Light soy sauce	2 Tbsp
Thai fish sauce	2 Tbsp
Sweet chilli sauce	2 Tbsp
Light brown sugar	1 Tbsp
Rice vinegar	2 Tbsp

METHOD

• Prepare sauce. Combine all sauce ingredients in a bowl and set aside.

• Heat oil in a wok. Add pork and fry until it browns, about 2–3 minutes. Add chopped chilli, bean sprouts and spring onions and stir-fry for 1 minute.

• Add noodles and sauce. Toss ingredients together and remove from heat. Transfer to a serving plate, garnish with peanuts and coriander and serve immediately.

vietnamese noodle salad with beef skewers

Serves 4

Known as *bun cha,* this is an everyday Vietnamese dish that is enjoyed with savoury barbecued beef or pork.

INGREDIENTS

Rice vinegar	90 ml (3 fl oz / $^3/_8$ cup)
Thai fish sauce	4 Tbsp
Sugar	1 Tbsp
Beef	600 g (1 lb $5^1/_3$ oz), trimmed of excess fat and cut into strips
Glass (transparent) noodles	200 g (7 oz)
Carrot	1, peeled and cut into thin sticks
Red chilli	1, thinly sliced
Mint leaves	30 g (1 oz)
Coriander leaves (cilantro)	45 g ($1^1/_2$ oz)

METHOD

• Soak 12 wooden skewers in cold water for 20 minutes.

• Mix 2 Tbsp vinegar with 1 Tbsp fish sauce and sugar in a bowl. Add beef and toss to coat. Cover and refrigerate for 10 minutes.

• Meanwhile, place noodles and carrot in a bowl and pour boiling water over. Let stand for a few minutes to soften, then drain.

• Combine noodles with chilli, mint, coriander and remaining fish sauce and vinegar. Toss and mix well. Transfer to a serving dish.

• Heat a lightly oiled grill over medium heat. While heating up, thread beef strips onto skewers. Grill or barbecue for 3–5 minutes until cooked through. Serve immediately with noodles.

gado gado (indonesian salad) Serves 4

This is an Indonesian salad of potato slices and cooked vegetables served with a rich peanut sauce.

INGREDIENTS

SALAD

Potatoes	2, boiled and sliced
Cabbage	1/4, shredded and steamed
Water convolvulus *(kangkong)*	100 g (3 1/2 oz), steamed
Bean sprouts	100 g (3 1/2 oz), scalded
Firm bean curd	2 cakes, deep-fried and cut into 1 x 2-cm (1/2 x 1-in) pieces
Cucumber	1/2, cut into rounds
Eggs	2, hard-boiled, peeled and sliced
Prawn crackers	a handful, deep-fried

SAUCE

Red chillies	8
Dried prawn (shrimp) paste *(belacan)*	1 tsp
Cooking oil	2 Tbsp
Shallots	8, peeled and finely sliced
Coconut milk	375 ml (12 fl oz / 1 1/2 cups)
Raw peanuts	70 g (2 1/2 oz), roasted and coarsely crushed, or 125 g (4 1/2 oz) crunchy peanut butter
Palm sugar or brown sugar	1–2 tsp
Tamarind juice	4 Tbsp, or 2 Tbsp lemon juice mixed with 2 Tbsp water
Salt	to taste

NOTE

The vegetables in this recipe should be lightly cooked so that they remain crisp.

To make tamarind juice, soak 1 Tbsp tamarind pulp in 4 Tbsp warm water for about 5 minutes. Mix well, then strain to remove any fibre and seeds.

METHOD

- Prepare sauce. Pound chillies and dried prawn paste together until a fine paste is achieved. Heat oil and sauté shallots or onion gently until soft. Add ground mixture and stir-fry for 4–5 minutes. Add coconut milk, a little at a time, then add all other ingredients for sauce. Simmer for about 3 minutes until sauce thickens. Set aside to cool to room temperature.

- Arrange salad ingredients in a deep serving dish. Just before serving, pour sauce over and toss lightly. Garnish with fried prawn crackers.

japanese potato salad Serves 4

This refreshing salad has a delicious dressing, comprising Japanese rice wine vinegar, olive oil and mayonnaise.

INGREDIENTS

Russet potatoes	450 g (1 lb)
Japanese rice wine vinegar	2 tsp
Olive oil	1 tsp
Salt	1/2 tsp
Japanese cucumber	1, halved lengthways, seeded and thinly sliced
Brown onion	1/2, peeled and thinly sliced
Ham	3 slices, cut into thin strips
Mayonnaise	4 Tbsp

METHOD

• Put potatoes into a pot of boiling salted water. Return to the boil, reduce heat and simmer for 15–20 minutes or until tender. Drain, peel and mash.

• When potatoes are still hot, add rice wine vinegar, olive oil and salt. Mix well. Leave aside to cool.

• Mix mashed potatoes, cucumber, onion and ham together with mayonnaise.

• Refrigerate to chill for an hour before serving. Garnish as desired.

noodle, mushroom and cabbage salad Serves 4

A filling appetiser or light lunch meal, this should be served hot, straight from the stove.

INGREDIENTS

Cooking oil	I Tbsp
Chinese cabbage	700 g (1 1/2 lb), thinly sliced
Ginger	2.5-cm (1-in) knob, peeled and minced
Garlic	2 cloves, peeled and minced
Dried Chinese mushrooms	12, soaked to soften, stems discarded and sliced
Light soy sauce	3 Tbsp
Egg noodles	500 g (1 lb 1 1/2 oz)
Sesame oil	85 ml (2 1/2 fl oz / 1/3 cup)
Lemon juice	2 Tbsp
Rice vinegar	I Tbsp
Sugar	2 tsp
Hard-boiled eggs	3, peeled; 2 thinly sliced, 1 chopped for garnish
Coriander leaves (cilantro)	200 g (7 oz), chopped
Roasted white sesame seeds	I Tbsp
Salt	to taste
Ground black pepper	to taste
Spring onions (scallions)	2, chopped

METHOD

- Heat oil in a wok over medium-high heat. Add cabbage, ginger, garlic and mushrooms. Stir-fry until cabbage wilts, for about 2 minutes. Remove from heat. Stir in 1 Tbsp soy sauce. Mix well.

- Cook noodles in a large pot of boiling salted water until just tender but still firm to the bite. Drain well and set aside in a large bowl.

- To make dressing, combine sesame oil, lemon juice, rice vinegar, sugar and remaining soy sauce in small bowl. Add dressing to noodles.

- Add sliced eggs, coriander and cabbage mixture. Toss well and season with salt and pepper.

- Sprinkle chopped spring onions, chopped egg and toasted sesame seeds over. Serve immediately.

flowering chives with soy bean sprouts Serves 4

This simple and nutritious dish can be served as part of a Chinese meal with white rice.

INGREDIENTS

Flowering chives	55 g (2 oz)
Soy bean sprouts	300 g (11 oz)
Cooking oil	2 Tbsp
Chopped garlic	$^1/_2$ Tbsp
Salt	$^1/_2$ tsp
Light soy sauce	1 Tbsp
Ground white pepper	$^1/_2$ tsp

METHOD

• Trim ends of chives and discard any yellowing stems. Wash, then cut chives into 2.5-cm (1-in) lengths.

• Pluck tails of soy bean sprouts, then wash and drain well in a colander.

• Heat oil in a wok and fry garlic until fragrant. Do not allow garlic to burn. Add chives and soy bean sprouts, then salt, soy sauce and pepper. Stir-fry over high heat for about 1 minute. Do not overcook the soy bean sprouts.

• Remove from heat and serve immediately.

cucumbers with mung bean sheets Serves 4

This simple dish can be served as an appetiser, or even as a snack with drinks.

INGREDIENTS

Japanese cucumbers	3, ends cut off
Garlic	4 cloves, peeled and minced
Salt	2 tsp
Sugar	2 Tbsp
Mung bean sheets	8 slices, soaked in cold water to soften, then cut into 2-cm (1-in) wide strips
Toasted white sesame seeds	

SEASONING

Sesame oil	1 Tbsp
White vinegar	1½ Tbsp

NOTE

If a spicy dish is preferred, substitute sesame oil with chilli oil and add 2–3 chopped red chillies.

METHOD

- Crush cucumbers slightly with a cleaver. Halve cucumbers lengthwise and cut into 2-cm (1-in) thick slices.

- Mix with garlic, salt and sugar. Put into a bowl, cover with plastic wrap and refrigerate for at least 4 hours. The salt will help to draw out water from cucumbers.

- Remove cucumbers from refrigerator, drain off excess water and mix with strips of mung bean sheets.

- Stir in seasoning, sprinkle with toasted sesame seeds and serve.

snow peas with mustard sauce Serves 4

As a variation to this recipe, snow peas may be substituted with fava beans or sugar peas.

INGREDIENTS

Snow peas	200 g (7 oz), trimmed
Finely sliced	
spring onion	
(scallion)	2 Tbsp

SEASONING

Salt	$^1/_2$ tsp
English mustard	3 Tbsp
Sesame oil	$^3/_4$ Tbsp

METHOD

- Blanch snow peas in simmering water for 5–8 minutes until cooked but still crunchy. Drain.

- Mix sliced spring onion with seasoning and stir into snow peas. Serve immediately.

french beans with sauce Serves 4

Plunging the cooked French beans into cold water will help preserve their fresh green colour. Choose French beans of a similar size for better presentation.

INGREDIENTS

French beans	300 g (11 oz), trimmed and cut into 9-cm (4$\frac{1}{2}$-in) lengths
Salt	1 tsp
Grated ginger	1 Tbsp
Sesame sauce (See Note)	4 Tbsp
Toasted white sesame seeds	

NOTE

To make sesame sauce, blend together: 2 Tbsp sesame paste, 2$\frac{1}{2}$ Tbsp light soy sauce, $\frac{1}{2}$ tsp salt, 4 Tbsp cold water, 1 tsp sugar and 1 Tbsp sesame oil. Ready-made sesame sauce can also be purchased in bottles from most Chinese grocery shops or supermarkets.

METHOD

- Cook French beans in boiling water with salt and grated ginger for 2–3 minutes. Drain and plunge immediately into a pan of iced water. Leave until beans are chilled.

- Drain well and mix with sesame sauce. Sprinkle with toasted sesame seeds and serve.

cucumber raita Serves 4

This cooling yoghurt dip is great served alongside hot and spicy dishes. It can also be served as a dip with crackers.

INGREDIENTS

Cucumber	1, medium, peeled and seeded
Plain yoghurt	250 ml (8 fl oz / 1 cup)
Green chilli	1
Curry leaves	1 stalk, plucked
Ground cumin	$1/4$ tsp
Salt	to taste

METHOD

• Grate cucumber, then place in a sieve to drain excess water. Set aside to drain while preparing rest of dish.

• Place remaining ingredients into a blender and blend until smooth. Spoon into a bowl.

• Add grated cucumber to yoghurt and mix. Refrigerate for at least 1 hour before serving with curries or tandoor-cooked meats.

shanghai salad Serves 4

There are many variations of Shanghai salad. Some include noodles and chicken breast.
This version is light and vegetarian.

INGREDIENTS

Baby corn	225 g (8 oz), halved if large
Snow peas	100 g (3½ oz)
Carrot	1 large, peeled and coarsely grated
Red capsicum (bell pepper)	1, small, cored, seeded and cut into thin strips
Onions	2, small, peeled and thinly sliced
White cabbage	450 g (1 lb), roughly chopped

DRESSING

Cooking oil	4 Tbsp
Lemon juice	1 Tbsp
Tomato sauce	1 Tbsp
Light soy sauce	½ tsp

METHOD

• Put baby corn in a small pot of water and bring to the boil, until tender-crisp. Drain and leave to cool.

• Blanch snow peas lightly in boiling water. Drain and leave to cool.

• Place baby corn and snow peas in a large salad bowl together with carrot, capsicum, onions and cabbage.

• Whisk together ingredients for dressing and pour over salad. Toss well and serve immediately.

rojak (malay fruit and vegetable salad) Serves 4–6

For this dish to be visually pleasing, cut the fruit and vegetables into pieces of a similar size.

INGREDIENTS

Pineapple	½, medium, peeled and cut into small pieces
Cucumber	1, medium, roll-cut into wedges
Turnip	1, medium, peeled and sliced
Bean sprouts	110 g (4 oz), tailed and blanched
Fried bean curd puffs	8, cut into small pieces
Crullers	2, cut into small pieces

SAUCE

Red chillies	3
Dried prawn (shrimp) paste (*belacan*)	2.5 x 2.5 x 1-cm (1 x 1 x ½-in) piece
Castor (superfine) sugar	3 tsp
Limes	4, juice extracted
Tamarind pulp	1 Tbsp, mixed with 100 ml (3½ fl oz) warm water and strained
Black prawn paste (*haeko*)	1 Tbsp
Raw peanuts	55 g (2 oz), roasted, skinned and finely pounded

METHOD

• Prepare sauce. Pound chillies and dried prawn paste together until fine. Combine with remaining ingredients into a paste.

• Toss fruit, vegetables, bean curd puffs and crullers in a bowl to mix well. Drizzle sauce over and toss well. Serve immediately.

pineapple and cucumber salad Serves 4–6

This simple salad is sweet, spicy and tangy all at the same time. Serve it as a side dish with other meat and vegetable dishes.

INGREDIENTS

Cucumbers	2, medium, cut into 2.5-cm (1-in) cubes
Pineapple	$\frac{1}{2}$, medium, peeled and cut into 2.5-cm (1-in) cubes
Dried prawns (shrimps)	4 Tbsp
Dried prawn (shrimp) paste (belacan)	1 x 1 x 0.5-cm ($\frac{1}{2}$ x $\frac{1}{2}$ x $\frac{1}{4}$-in) piece, toasted
Red chillies	4
Lime juice	4 Tbsp
Palm sugar	1 Tbsp

METHOD

• Place cucumbers and pineapple in a mixing bowl. Refrigerate for at least 1 hour to chill.

• Soak dried prawns in hot water for 20 minutes to soften. Drain well and pound together with prawn paste and chillies until fine. Add lime juice, salt and sugar and mix well. Refrigerate for at least 1 hour to chill.

• Drizzle chilled sauce over cucumbers and pineapple. Toss well. Serve cold.

pecal Serves 4–6

This Malay dish of boiled vegetables with peanut sauce is simple to put together. It is usually served as a side dish, but can also be enjoyed on its own as a light meal.

INGREDIENTS

Sweet potato leaves	180 g (6$^1/_2$ oz), fibrous skin removed
Spinach	180 g (6$^1/_2$ oz), cut into 3-cm (1$^1/_2$-in) lengths
Long beans	4, cut into 3-cm (1$^1/_2$-in) lengths
White cabbage	4 leaves, cut into 3 x 3-cm (1$^1/_2$ x 1$^1/_2$-in) squares
Dried chillies	10, soaked in hot water to soften
Shallots	8, peeled
Tamarind pulp	1 Tbsp, mixed with 4 Tbsp water and strained
Dried prawn (shrimp) paste (*belacan*)	2.5 x 2.5 x 1-cm (1 x 1 x $^1/_2$-in) piece
Cooking oil	2 Tbsp
Raw peanuts	100 g (3$^1/_2$ oz), roasted, skinned and finely ground
Palm sugar	4 Tbsp
Prawn crackers	a handful, deep-fried

METHOD

• Bring a large pot of water to the boil. Add some salt, then plunge sweet potato leaves, spinach, long beans and cabbage in to cook lightly. Drain well and set aside.

• Place softened dried chillies, shallots, tamarind liquid and dried prawn paste into a blender and blend into a fine paste.

• Heat oil and fry paste until fragrant. Stir in peanuts, palm sugar and salt. Remove from heat.

• Drizzle gravy over vegetables and garnish with prawn crackers. Serve.

nasi kerabu Serves 6–8

This tossed rice salad originates from Kelantan, Malaysia. It is served at room temperature.

INGREDIENTS

Cooked long-grain rice	800 g (1 3/4 lb)

SAMBAL

Grated skinned coconut	200 g (7 oz)
Mackerel	1
Ground black pepper	1/4 tsp
Salt	1/4 tsp
Grated palm sugar	1 tsp

SPICE PASTE

Onions	10, small, peeled
Garlic	2 cloves, peeled
Dried chillies	10, soaked to soften
Dried prawn (shrimp) paste (*belacan*)	2.5 × 2.5 × 1-cm (1 × 1 × 1/2-in)
Coconut milk	125 ml (4 fl oz / 1/2 cup)
Lemon grass	1 stalk, bruised
Dried sour fruit (*asam gelugur*)	2 slices
Grated palm sugar	1 Tbsp
Salt	1/4 tsp

SALAD

Polygonum (*laksa*) leaves	4, finely sliced
Long beans	5, finely sliced
Lemon grass	1 stalk, white part only, finely sliced
Bean sprouts	110 g (4 oz), tailed

METHOD

- Prepare sambal. Dry-fry grated coconut until light brown. Set aside. Heat some oil in a pan and cook mackerel until well done. Flake flesh finely and discard bones, head and tail. Mix fish with grated coconut and remaining sambal ingredients.

- Prepare paste. Blend together onions, garlic, chillies and dried prawn paste. Place in a pan with coconut milk and bring to the boil. Lower heat and add lemon grass, dried sour fruit slices, palm sugar and salt. Simmer until sauce is thick.

- Serve sambal, spice paste and salad on the side with cooked rice. Allow guests to mix the ingredients together for themselves before eating.

sambal fish roe Serves 4–6

This cooked fish roe dish goes well with plain rice. Serve as part of a meal with other meat and vegetable dishes.

INGREDIENTS

Fish roe	600 g (1 lb 5$^{1}/_{3}$ oz)
Cooking oil	4 Tbsp
Limes	4, cut into wedges
Salt	$^{1}/_{8}$ tsp
Sugar	1 tsp

SPICE PASTE

Red chillies	6, seeded
Shallots	6, peeled
Candlenuts	4
Garlic	2 cloves, peeled
Turmeric	1-cm ($^{1}/_{2}$-in) knob, peeled

METHOD

- Steam fish roe until cooked. Takes about 15 minutes. Leave to cool, then pat dry before frying.

- Heat 2 Tbsp oil in a wok and fry fish roe on both sides until brown and crisp. Drain and mash. Set aside.

- Place ingredients for spice paste in a blender and blend until fine. Heat remaining oil in a clean wok and fry paste until fragrant. Add fish roe and mix well. Season with salt and sugar.

- Transfer to a serving plate and serve with lime wedges on the side.

spicy fish salad Serves 4

This traditional Thai salad can be served as part of a Thai meal, as a sandwich filling, or as a dip with crackers.

INGREDIENTS

Catfish or mackerel	1, medium
Cooking oil	500 ml (16 fl oz / 2 cups)
Green mango	1, large, peeled and cut into thin strips
Brown sugar	2 Tbsp
Thai fish sauce	2 Tbsp
Bird's eye chillies	4, finely sliced
Shallots	6, peeled and finely sliced
Raw peanuts	70 g (2½ oz), roasted, skinned and coarsely pounded
Coriander leaves (cilantro)	

METHOD

• Steam fish until done. Remove and leave to cool. When fish is cool, flake flesh. Discard skin and bones.

• Heat oil over medium heat and deep-fry fish flakes until golden brown. Remove using a wire strainer and set aside on paper towels to cool and drain of oil.

• Place fish in a mixing bowl with mango, sugar, fish sauce, bird's eye chillies, shallots and peanuts. Toss well to mix.

• Serve, garnished with coriander leaves.

cold cucumber and wakame salad Serves 4

This cold Japanese salad can be served as a side dish to refresh the palate between courses.

INGREDIENTS

Japanese cucumbers	2
Salt	$\frac{1}{2}$ tsp
Wakame	
(dried seaweed)	30 g (1 oz)

DRESSING

Japanese rice	
vinegar	4 Tbsp
Japanese light	
soy sauce	4 Tbsp
Sesame oil	1 Tbsp
Sugar	1 Tbsp

METHOD

• Prepare dressing. Combine all ingredients in a pan and place over gentle heat, stirring to dissolve sugar. Remove from heat and set aside to cool.

• Cut cucumbers in half lengthwise, then scoop out the soft centres. Cut into fine strips and place in a bowl. Sprinkle with salt and leave for 30 minutes. Drain, then place cucumber strips on a clean, dry kitchen towel and squeeze to remove excess moisture. Place in a salad bowl.

• Soak wakame in a bowl of warm water for about 20 minutes, or until seaweed expands. Rinse and pat dry. Cut into small pieces.

• Place wakame in bowl with cucumber strips. Drizzle dressing over and toss to coat well.

• Serve chilled.

daikon and carrot in vinegar dressing Serves 4

This simple daikon (white) and carrot (red) salad spots the colours that the Japanese regard as representative of happiness and celebration, and is thus popularly served as part of the New Year's meal in Japan.

INGREDIENTS

Daikon (white radish)	450 g (1 lb)
Carrots	280 g (10 oz)

DRESSING

Salt	1 tsp
Sugar	3 Tbsp
Japanese rice vinegar	85 ml (2$\frac{1}{2}$ fl oz / $\frac{1}{3}$ cup)

METHOD

• Prepare salad a day ahead.

• Peel daikon, then cut into 5-cm (2-in) sections before cutting into fine strips. Repeat with carrots.

• Place in a large bowl and sprinkle with salt. Toss, then leave for 30 minutes. Drain and place vegetables on a clean, dry kitchen towel and squeeze to remove excess moisture. Place in a bowl.

• Combine ingredients for dressing and stir to dissolve sugar and salt. Pour over vegetables. Leave for a day in a cool place, tossing 2–3 times to mix ingredients.

• Toss vegetables again just before serving.

grilled aubergine salad Serves 4

There are many versions of aubergine salad, and this Burmese recipe combines a few other typical Asian ingredients such as sesame seeds, bird's eye chillies and fish sauce to make a delicious salad.

INGREDIENTS

Aubergines (eggplants/ brinjals)	2, medium
Cooking oil	2 Tbsp
Garlic	4 cloves, peeled and finely sliced
Onion	1, medium, peeled and finely sliced
Raw peanuts	2 Tbsp, roasted, skinned and roughly chopped
White sesame seeds	1 Tbsp, toasted
Bird's eye chillies	2, finely sliced
Thai fish sauce	2 tsp

METHOD

• Grill aubergines until skin is slightly charred. Leave to cool, then peel and discard skin. Mash flesh and place in a mixing bowl.

• Heat oil in a wok and fry garlic until crisp and golden. Remove and drain well. Reserve $\frac{1}{2}$ Tbsp garlic oil.

• Add garlic, onion, peanuts, sesame seeds, chillies, fish sauce and garlic oil to mashed aubergine in mixing bowl. Mix well.

• Dish out and serve.

filipino-style fruit salad Serves 6

Serve this as a dessert after a meal, or as a refreshing pick-me-up at any time of the day.

INGREDIENTS

Cream cheese	125 g (4$\frac{1}{2}$ oz), softened at room temperature
Sweetened condensed milk	125 g (4$\frac{1}{2}$ oz)
Fruit cocktail	2 cans, each 425 g (14$\frac{1}{3}$ oz), well drained
Seedless purple grapes	100 g (3$\frac{1}{2}$ oz)
Nata de coco	100 g (3$\frac{1}{2}$ oz), well drained
Almonds	1 Tbsp, roasted and roughly chopped

METHOD

- Beat cream cheese and condensed milk together into a smooth sauce. Set aside.

- Combine fruit cocktail, grapes and nata de coco in a mixing bowl. Drizzle cream cheese sauce over and refrigerate for 30–45 minutes to chill.

- Sprinkle with almonds and serve.

weights and measures

Quantities for this book are given in Metric, Imperial and American (spoon and cup) measures. Standard spoon and cup measurements used are: 1 tsp = 5 ml, 1 Tbsp = 15 ml, 1 cup = 250 ml. All measures are level unless otherwise stated.

Liquid And Volume Measures

Metric	Imperial	American
5 ml	1/6 fl oz	1 teaspoon
10 ml	1/3 fl oz	1 dessertspoon
15 ml	1/2 fl oz	1 tablespoon
60 ml	2 fl oz	1/4 cup (4 tablespoons)
85 ml	2 1/2 fl oz	1/3 cup
90 ml	3 fl oz	3/8 cup (6 tablespoons)
125 ml	4 fl oz	1/2 cup
180 ml	6 fl oz	3/4 cup
250 ml	8 fl oz	1 cup
300 ml	10 fl oz (1/2 pint)	1 1/4 cups
375 ml	12 fl oz	1 1/2 cups
435 ml	14 fl oz	1 3/4 cups
500 ml	16 fl oz	2 cups
625 ml	20 fl oz (1 pint)	2 1/2 cups
750 ml	24 fl oz (1 1/5 pints)	3 cups
1 litre	32 fl oz (1 3/5 pints)	4 cups
1.25 litres	40 fl oz (2 pints)	5 cups
1.5 litres	48 fl oz (2 2/5 pints)	6 cups
2.5 litres	80 fl oz (4 pints)	10 cups

Dry Measures

Metric	Imperial
30 grams	1 ounce
45 grams	1 1/2 ounces
55 grams	2 ounces
70 grams	2 1/2 ounces
85 grams	3 ounces
100 grams	3 1/2 ounces
110 grams	4 ounces
125 grams	4 1/2 ounces
140 grams	5 ounces
280 grams	10 ounces
450 grams	16 ounces (1 pound)
500 grams	1 pound, 1 1/2 ounces
700 grams	1 1/2 pounds
800 grams	1 3/4 pounds
1 kilogram	2 pounds, 3 ounces
1.5 kilograms	3 pounds, 4 1/2 ounces
2 kilograms	4 pounds, 6 ounces

Oven Temperature

	°C	°F	Gas Regulo
Very slow	120	250	1
Slow	150	300	2
Moderately slow	160	325	3
Moderate	180	350	4
Moderately hot	190/200	375/400	5/6
Hot	210/220	410/425	6/7
Very hot	230	450	8
Super hot	250/290	475/550	9/10

Length

Metric	Imperial
0.5 cm	1/4 inch
1 cm	1/2 inch
1.5 cm	3/4 inch
2.5 cm	1 inch

Abbreviation

tsp	teaspoon
Tbsp	tablespoon
g	gram
kg	kilogram
ml	millilitre